Popular Hits
BOOK 1

Arranged by Fred Kern · Phillip Keveren · Mona Rejino

Edited by J. Mark Baker

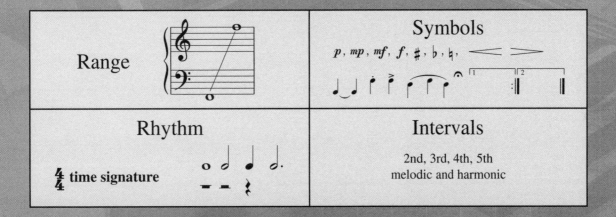

Range	Symbols
	p, mp, mf, f, ♯, ♭, ♮
Rhythm	**Intervals**
$\frac{4}{4}$ time signature	2nd, 3rd, 4th, 5th melodic and harmonic

To access audio visit:
www.halleonard.com/mylibrary

Enter Code
5543-4978-9336-0971

ISBN 978-0-634-08745-5

HAL•LEONARD®
CORPORATION

7777 W. BLUEMOUND RD. P.O. BOX 13819 MILWAUKEE, WI 53213

Visit Hal Leonard Online at
www.halleonard.com

Popular Hits

BOOK 1

Suggested Order of Study:

Strangers in the Night

The Way You Look Tonight

Circle of Life

My Heart Will Go On
(Love Theme from 'Titanic')

Sing

Y.M.C.A.

Fun, Fun, Fun

The Music of the Night

Let It Be Me

Vincent (Starry Starry Night)

American Pie

Murder, She Wrote

Full orchestrated arrangements are included with this book and may be used for both practice and performance. There are two accompaniment tracks for each piece. The first is a practice tempo; it is slower and includes the piano melody. The second is the performance tempo—a little faster—and without the piano melody.

To access the accompanying audio and MIDI files, simply go to **www.halleonard.com/mylibrary** and enter the code found on page 1 of this book. This will grant you instant access to every file. You can download to your computer, tablet, or phone, or stream the audio live—and if your device has Flash, you can also use our *PLAYBACK+* multi-functional audio player to slow down or speed up the tempo, change keys, or set loop points. This feature is available exclusively from Hal Leonard and is included with the price of this book!

For technical support, please email **support@halleonard.com**.

Contents

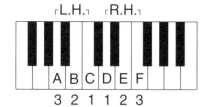

Strangers in the Night
adapted from A MAN COULD GET KILLED

Words by Charles Singleton and Eddie Snyder
Music by Bert Kaempfert
Arranged by Phillip Keveren

Tenderly (♩ = 80)

mp Stran - gers in the night, _____ ex - chang - ing glanc - es,

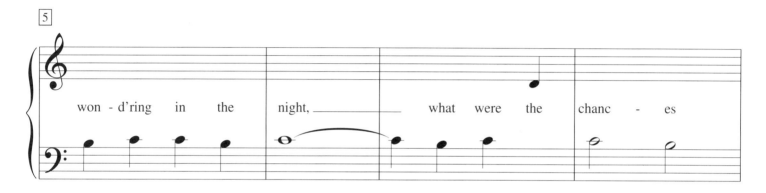

won - d'ring in the night, _____ what were the chanc - es

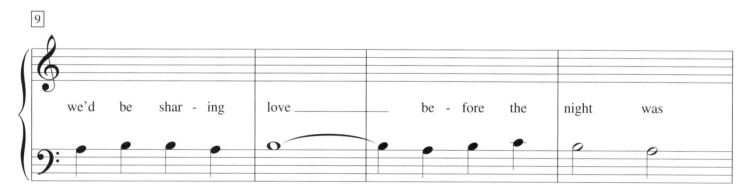

we'd be shar - ing love _____ be - fore the night was

Accompaniment (Student plays one octave higher than written.)

Tenderly (♩ = 80)

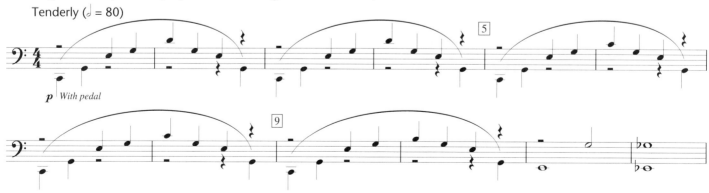

p With pedal

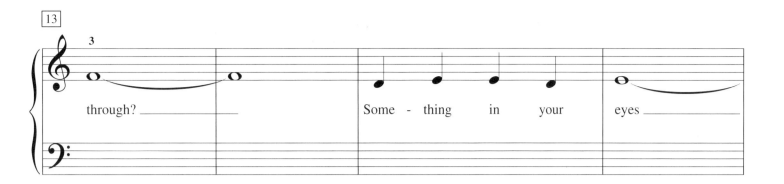

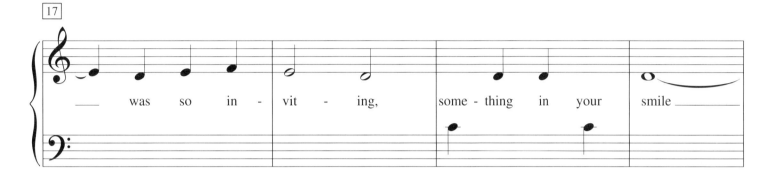

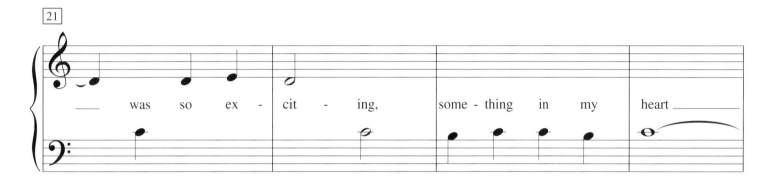

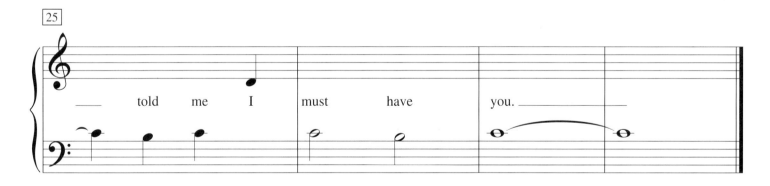

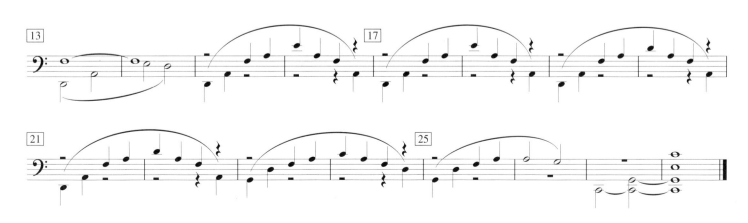

The Way You Look Tonight

from SWING TIME

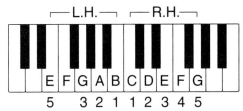

Words by Dorothy Fields
Music by Jerome Kern
Arranged by Fred Kern

Moderately (♩ = 120)

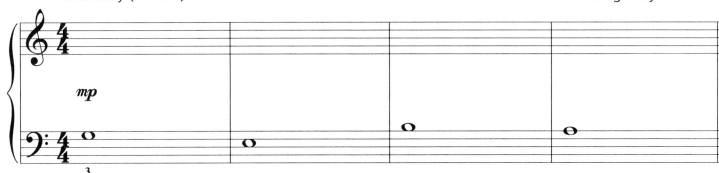

Some - day when I'm aw - f'lly low,
love - ly with your smile so warm,

Accompaniment (Student plays one octave higher than written.)

Moderately (♩ = 120)

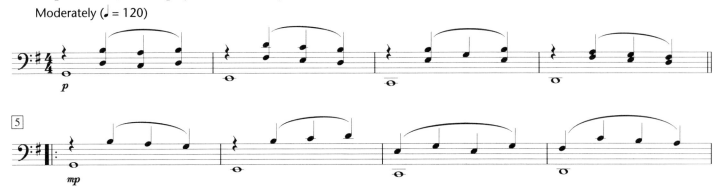

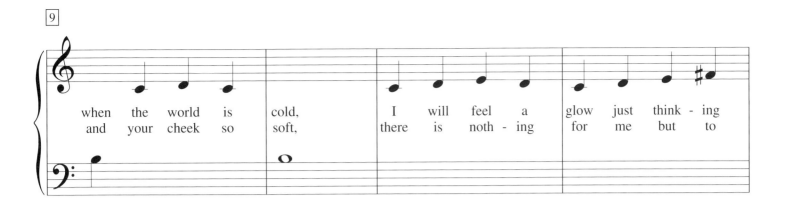

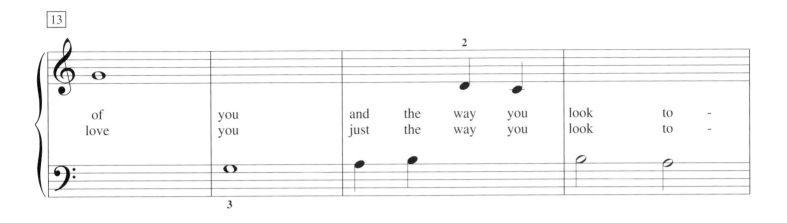

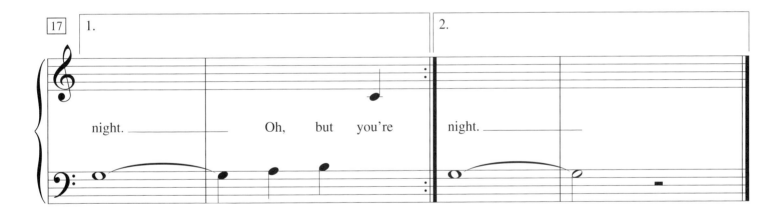

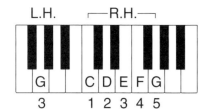

Circle of Life

from Walt Disney Pictures' THE LION KING

Music by Elton John
Lyrics by Tim Rice
Arranged by Fred Kern

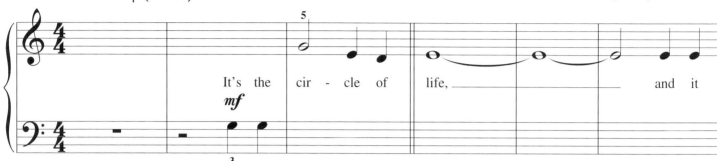

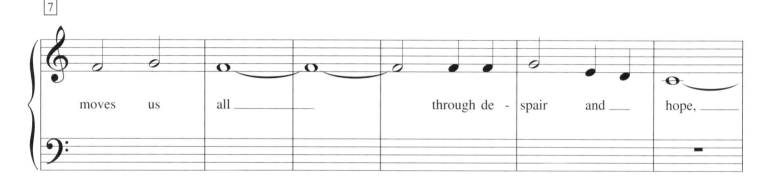

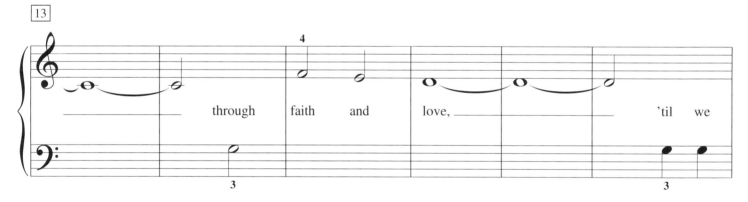

Accompaniment (Student plays one octave higher than written.)

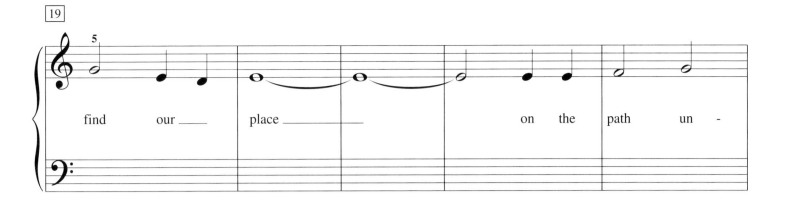

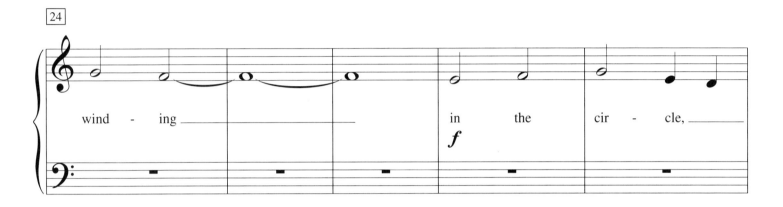

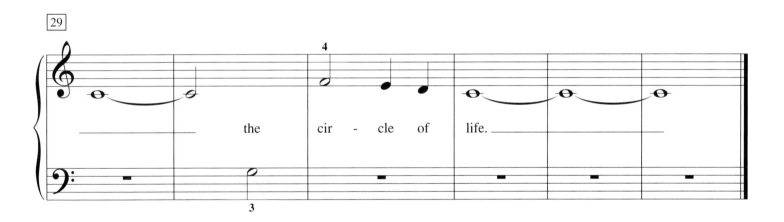

My Heart Will Go On

(Love Theme from 'Titanic')

from the Paramount and Twentieth Century Fox Motion Picture TITANIC

Music by James Horner
Lyric by Will Jennings
Arranged by Phillip Keveren

Ev - 'ry night in my dreams I see you, I feel you,
Far a - cross the dis - tance and spac - es be - tween us,

* = may be played

that is how I know you go on.
you have come to show you go on.

Accompaniment (Student plays one octave higher than written.)

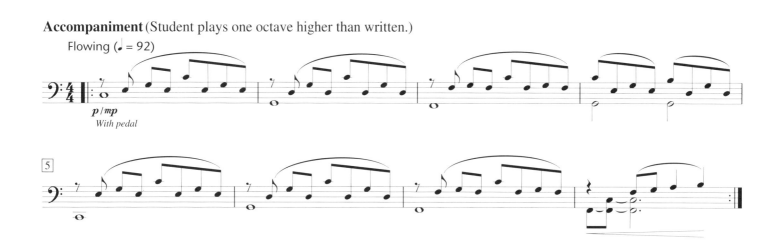

With pedal

Sing

from SESAME STREET

Words and Music by Joe Raposo
Arranged by Fred Kern

Lively, in "two" (♩ = 80)

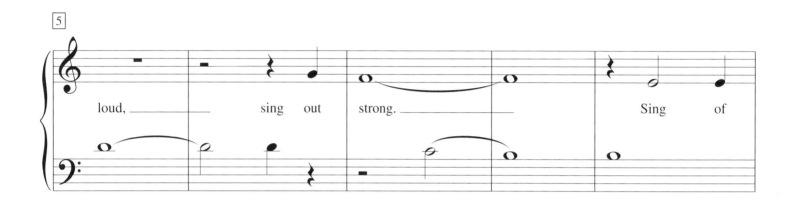

Sing! _____ Sing a song. _____ Sing out

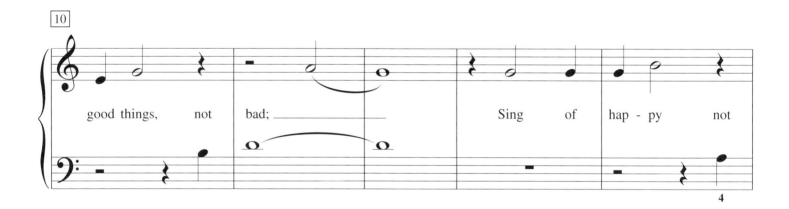

loud, _____ sing out strong. _____ Sing of

good things, not bad; _____ Sing of hap - py not

Accompaniment (Student plays one octave higher than written.)

Lively, in "two" (♩ = 80)

Y.M.C.A.

Words and Music by Jacques Morali,
Henri Belolo and Victor Willis
Arranged by Phillip Keveren

Y. M. C. A.

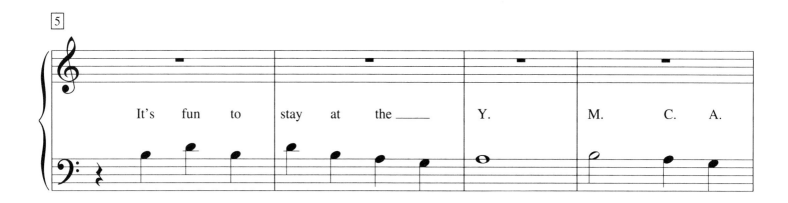

It's fun to stay at the ___ Y. M. C. A.

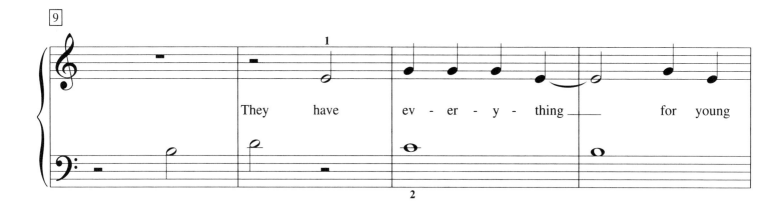

They have ev-er-y-thing ___ for young

Accompaniment (Student plays one octave higher than written.)

Bright Disco (♩ = 100)

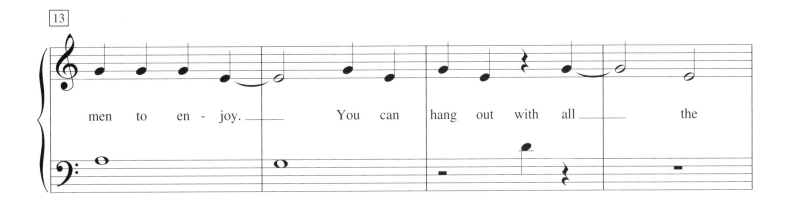

men to en - joy. _____ You can hang out with all _____ the

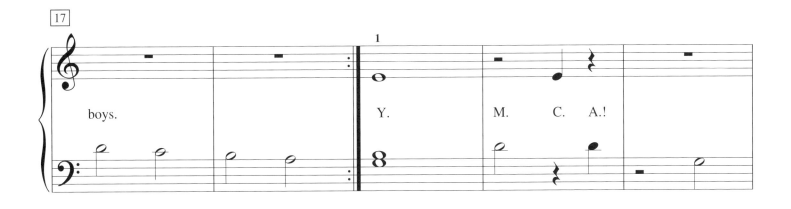

boys.

Y. M. C. A.!

Y. M. C. A.!

Fun, Fun, Fun

Words and Music by
Brian Wilson and Mike Love
Arranged by Mona Rejino

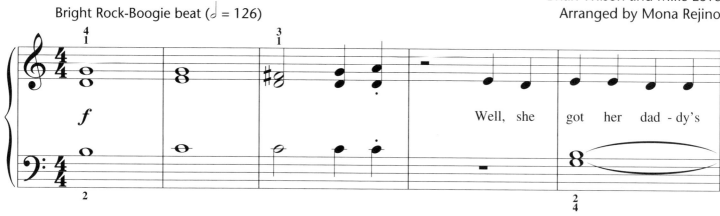

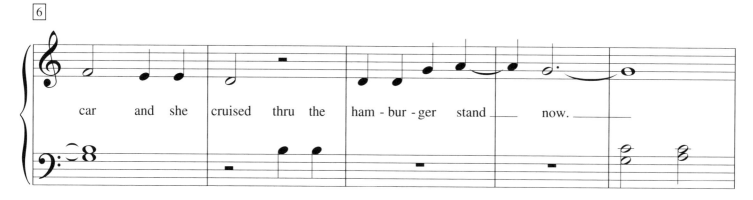

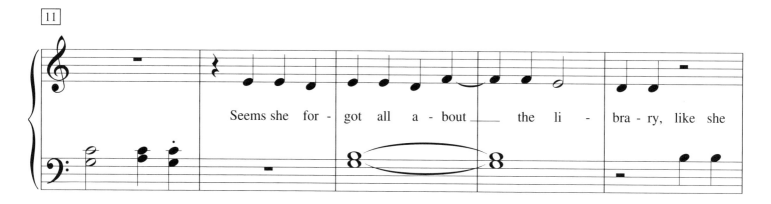

Accompaniment (Student plays one octave higher than written.)

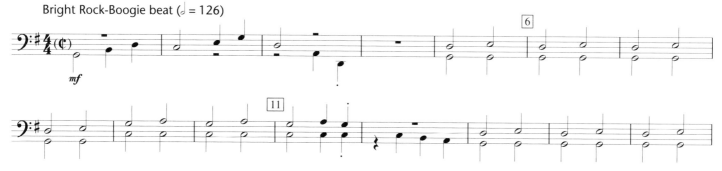

told her "old man" _____ now. _____

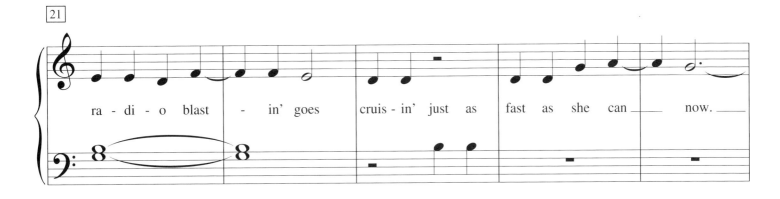

ra - di - o blast - in' goes cruis - in' just as fast as she can _____ now. _____

_____ And she'll have fun, fun, fun, till her dad - dy takes the

"T - Bird" a - way. _____

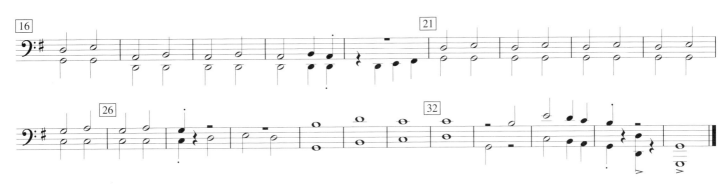

The Music of the Night
from THE PHANTOM OF THE OPERA

Music by Andrew Lloyd Webber
Lyrics by Charles Hart
Additional Lyrics by Richard Stilgoe
Arranged by Mona Rejino

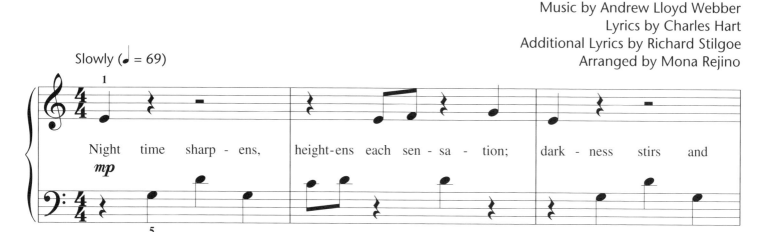

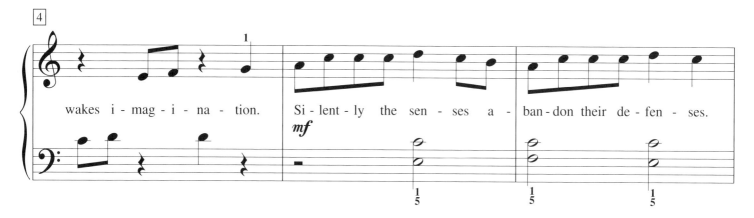

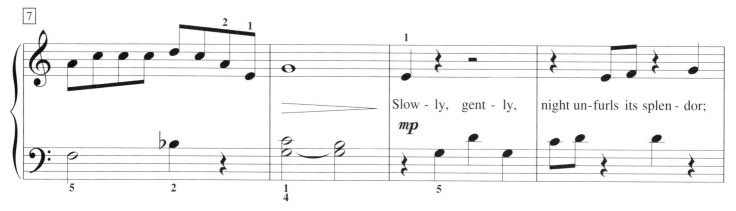

Accompaniment (Student plays one octave higher than written.)

19

Let It Be Me

English Words by Mann Curtis
French Words by Pierre DeLanoe
Music by Gilbert Becaud
Arranged by Mona Rejino

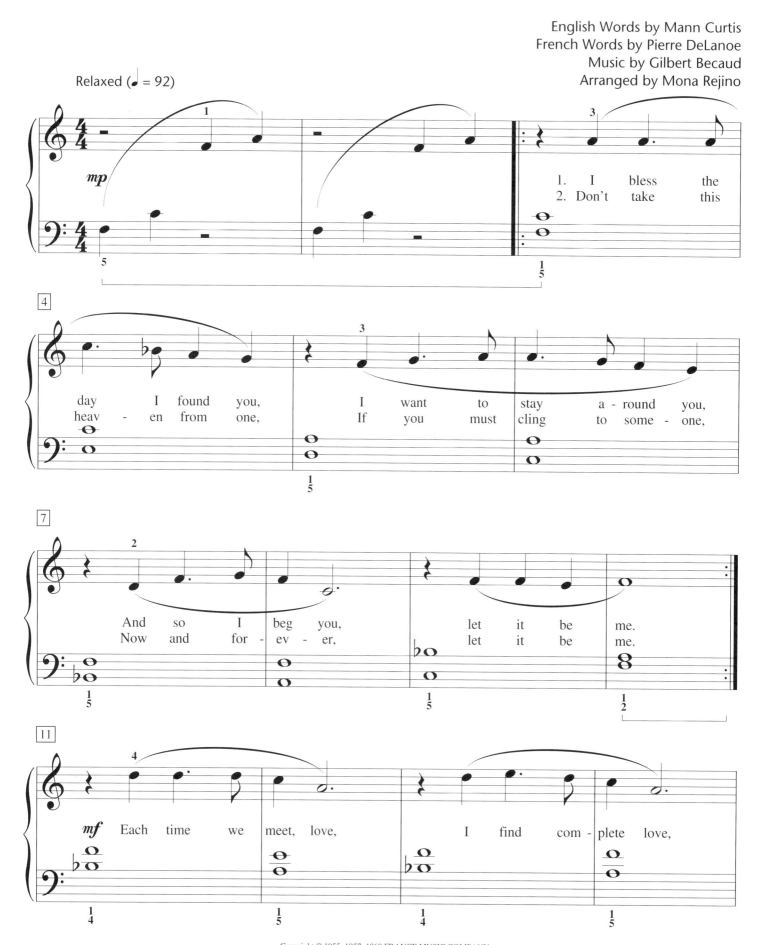

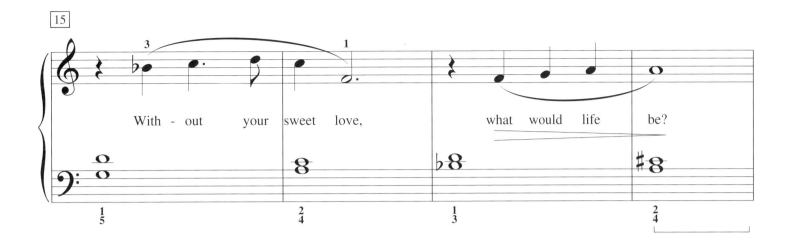

With - out your sweet love, what would life be?

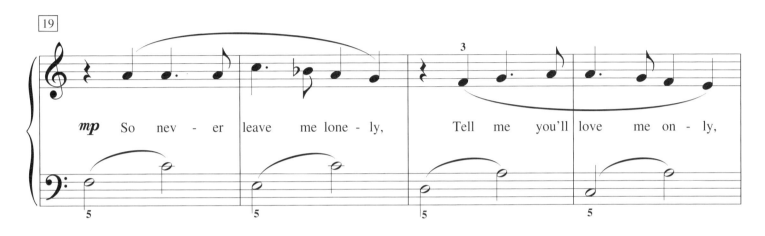

mp So nev - er leave me lone - ly, Tell me you'll love me on - ly,

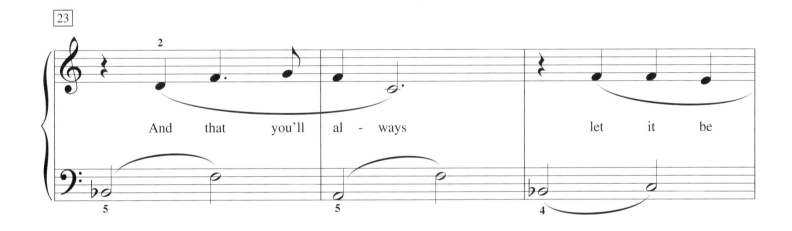

And that you'll al - ways let it be

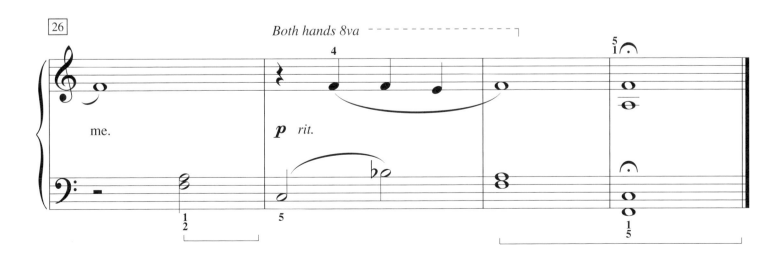

me. *p* *rit.*

Both hands 8va

American Pie

Words and Music by Don McLean
Arranged by Phillip Keveren

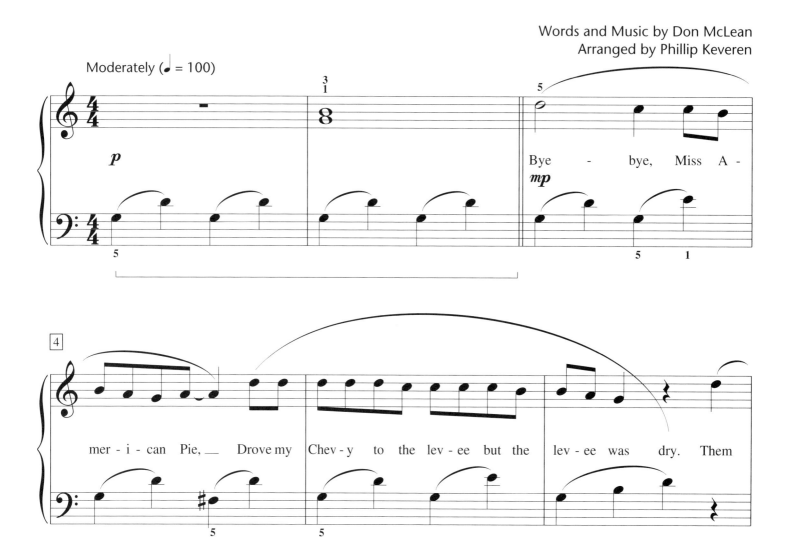

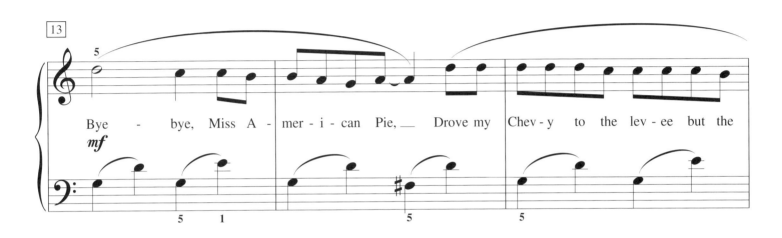

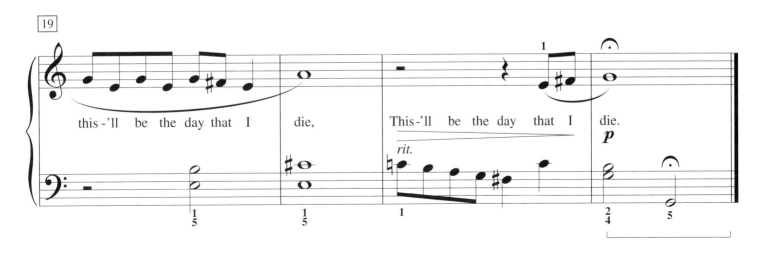

Murder, She Wrote

Theme from the Universal Television Series MURDER, SHE WROTE

Music by John Addison
Arranged by Phillip Keveren

Allegro (♩ = 104)

Vincent
(Starry Starry Night)

Words and Music by Don McLean
Arranged by Fred Kern

Moderately (♩ = 96)

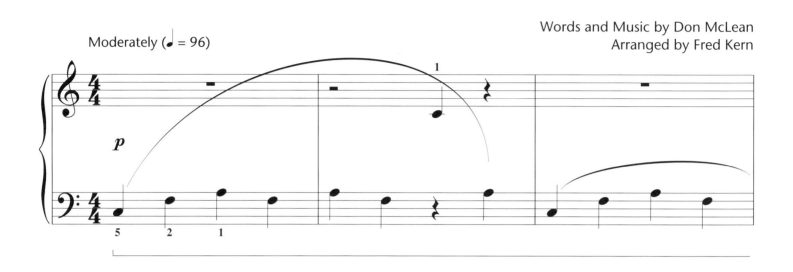

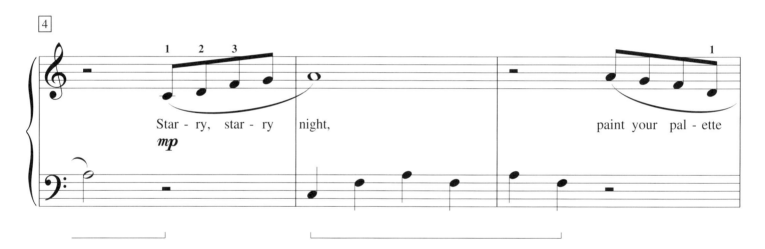

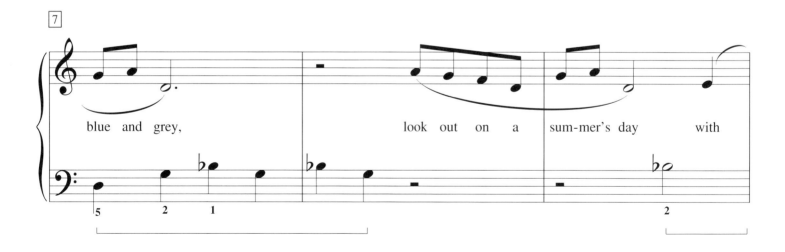

eyes that know the dark-ness in my soul. Shad-ows on the hills,

mf

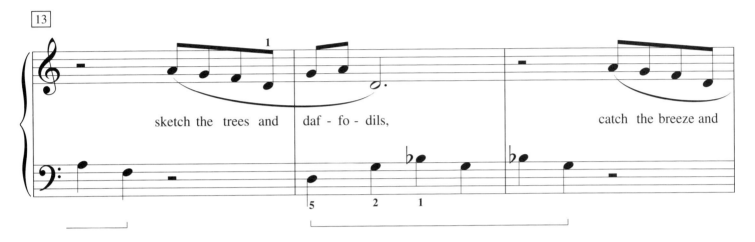

sketch the trees and daf - fo - dils, catch the breeze and

win - ter chills in col - ors on the snow - y lin - en land._____

_____ Star - ry, star - ry night, flam - ing flowers that

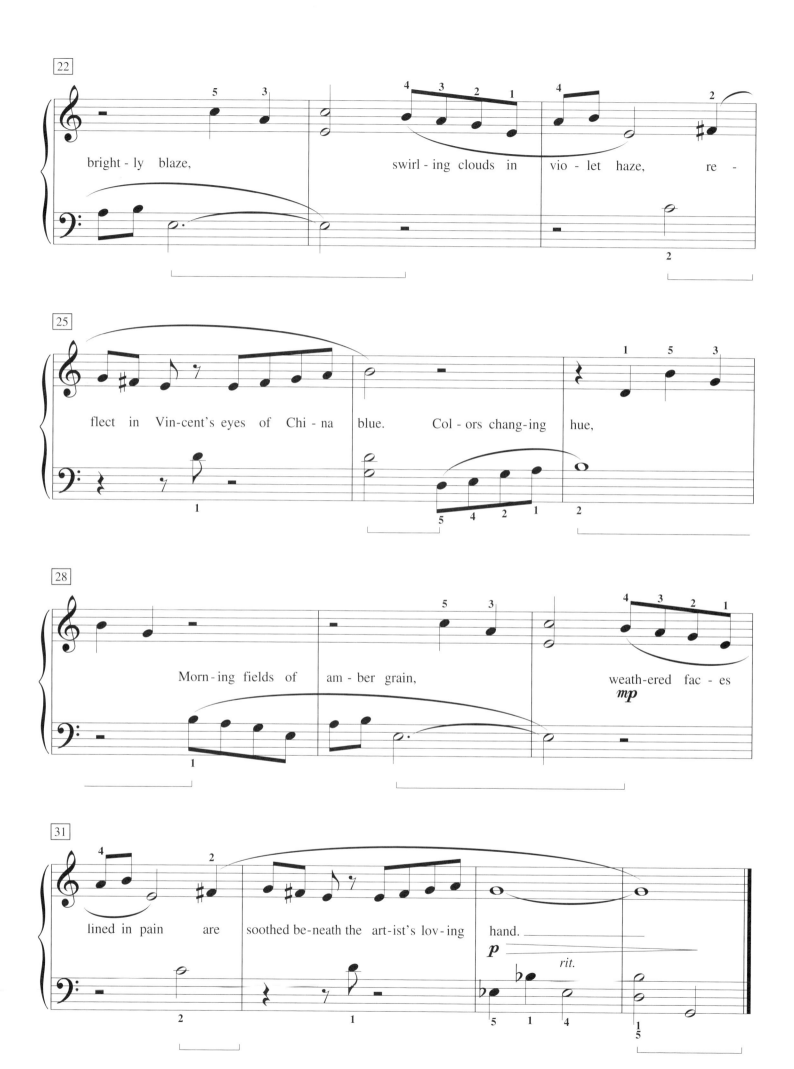

bright - ly blaze,   swirl - ing clouds in   vio - let haze,   re -

flect in Vin-cent's eyes of Chi - na blue.   Col - ors chang-ing   hue,

Morn-ing fields of   am - ber grain,   weath-ered fac - es
mp

lined in pain   are   soothed be-neath the art-ist's lov-ing   hand.
p   *rit.*

Hal Leonard Student Piano Library

Adult Piano Method

Adult Piano Method

Adults want to play rewarding music and enjoy their piano study. They deserve a method that lives up to those expectations. The *Hal Leonard Student Piano Library Adult Piano Method* does just that and more.

Method Book 1
00296441 Book/Online Audio $16.99

Method Book 2
00296480 Book/Online Audio $16.99

Popular Hits Book 1

Our hit-packed supplementary songbook includes these titles: American Pie • Circle of Life • Fun, Fun, Fun • Let It Be Me • Murder, She Wrote • The Music of the Night • My Heart Will Go On • Sing • Strangers in the Night • Vincent (Starry Starry Night) • Y.M.C.A. • The Way You Look Tonight.
00296541 Book/Online Audio $12.99

Popular Hits Book 2

12 hits: I Will Remember You • I Wish You Love • I Write the Songs • In the Mood • Moon River • Oh, Pretty Woman • The Phantom of the Opera • Stand by Me • Tears in Heaven • Unchained Melody • What a Wonderful World • When I'm Sixty-Four.
00296652 Book/Online Audio $12.99

Popular Favorites Book 1

11 favorites: Are You Lonesome Tonight? • Bless the Broken Road • Don't Know Why • Every Breath You Take • From a Distance • Help Me Make It Through the Night • I Hope You Dance • Imagine • Lean on Me • The Nearness of You • Right Here Waiting.
00296826 Book/Enhanced CD Pack.....................................$12.99

Popular Favorites Book 2

12 classics: All I Have to Do Is Dream • Georgia on My Mind • I Just Called to Say I Love You • I'm a Believer • Memory • Never on a Sunday • On My Own • One Fine Day • Satin Doll • That'll Be the Day • We Are the World • Your Song.
00296842 Book/Enhanced CD Pack.....................................$12.99

Christmas Favorites Book 1

12 favorites: Away in a Manger • Deck the Hall • God Rest Ye Merry, Gentlemen • I Saw Three Ships • Jingle Bells • Joy to the World • O Come, O Come, Emmanuel • O Little Town of Bethleham • Silent Night • Ukrainian Bell Carol • We Wish You a Merry Christmas • What Child Is This?
00296544 Book/CD Pack...$12.99

Christmas Favorites Book 2

12 more holiday classics: Angels We Have Heard on High • Bring a Torch, Jeannette Isabella • Dance of the Sugar Plum Fairy • Ding Dong! Merrily on High! • The First Noel • Go, Tell It on the Mountain • Hark! The Herald Angels Sing • The Holly and the Ivy • O Christmas Tree • O Holy Night • Still, Still, Still • We Three Kings of Orient Are.
00296668 Book/CD Pack...$12.99

Traditional Hymns Book 1

16 sacred favorites: All Glory, Laud and Honor • Come, Thou Almighty King • For the Beauty of the Earth • Holy, Holy, Holy! • It Is Well with My Soul • Joyful, Joyful, We Adore Thee • A Mighty Fortress Is Our God • What a Friend We Have in Jesus • and more.
00296782 Book/CD Pack...$12.99

Traditional Hymns Book 2

15 more traditional hymns: All Things Bright and Beautiful • Ezekiel Saw the Wheel • God of Grace and God of Glory • God Will Take Care of You • In the Garden • Lord, I Want to Be a Christian • Stand Up, Stand Up for Jesus • Swing Low, Sweet Chariot • This Is My Father's World • and more.
00296783 Book/CD Pack...$12.99

Prices, contents and availability are subject to change without notice.

FOR MORE INFORMATION, SEE YOUR LOCAL MUSIC DEALER, OR WRITE TO:

HAL•LEONARD® CORPORATION

7777 W. BLUEMOUND RD. P.O. BOX 13819 MILWAUKEE, WI 53213

www.halleonard.com

COMPOSER SHOWCASE
HAL LEONARD STUDENT PIANO LIBRARY

This series showcases great original piano music from our **Hal Leonard Student Piano Library** family of composers, including Bill Boyd, Phillip Keveren, Carol Klose, Jennifer Linn, Mona Rejino, Eugénie Rocherolle and more. Carefully graded for easy selection, each book contains gems that are certain to become tomorrow's classics!

BILL BOYD

JAZZ BITS (AND PIECES)
Early Intermediate Level
00290312 11 Solos......................................$7.99

JAZZ DELIGHTS
Intermediate Level
00240435 11 Solos......................................$7.99

JAZZ FEST
Intermediate Level
00240436 10 Solos......................................$7.99

JAZZ PRELIMS
Early Elementary Level
00290032 12 Solos......................................$6.99

JAZZ SKETCHES
Intermediate Level
00220001 8 Solos..$7.99

JAZZ STARTERS
Elementary Level
00290425 10 Solos......................................$7.99

JAZZ STARTERS II
Late Elementary Level
00290434 11 Solos......................................$7.99

JAZZ STARTERS III
Late Elementary Level
00290465 12 Solos......................................$7.99

THINK JAZZ!
Early Intermediate Level
00290417 Method Book..............................$10.99

TONY CARAMIA

JAZZ MOODS
Intermediate Level
00296728 8 Solos..$6.95

SUITE DREAMS
Intermediate Level
00296775 4 Solos..$6.99

SONDRA CLARK

FAVORITE CAROLS FOR TWO
Intermediate Level
00296530 5 Duets.......................................$7.99

THREE ODD METERS
Intermediate Level
00296472 3 Duets.......................................$6.95

MATTHEW EDWARDS

CONCERTO FOR YOUNG PIANISTS
FOR 2 PIANOS, FOUR HANDS
Intermediate Level Book/CD
00296356 3 Movements $16.95

CONCERTO NO. 2 IN G MAJOR
FOR 2 PIANOS, 4 HANDS
Intermediate Level Book/CD
00296670 3 Movements..............................$16.95

PHILLIP KEVEREN

MOUSE ON A MIRROR
Late Elementary Level
00296361 5 Solos..$6.95

MUSICAL MOODS
Elementary/Late Elementary Level
00296714 7 Solos..$5.95

SHIFTY-EYED BLUES
Late Elementary Level
00296374 5 Solos..$6.99

TEX-MEX REX
Late Elementary Level
00296353 6 Solos..$6.99

CAROL KLOSE

THE BEST OF CAROL KLOSE
Early Intermediate to Late Intermediate Level
00146151 15 Solos.....................................$12.99

CORAL REEF SUITE
Late Elementary Level
00296354 7 Solos..$6.99

DESERT SUITE
Intermediate Level
00296667 6 Solos..$7.99

FANCIFUL WALTZES
Early Intermediate Level
00296473 5 Solos..$7.95

GARDEN TREASURES
Late Intermediate Level
00296787 5 Solos..$7.99

ROMANTIC EXPRESSIONS
Intermediate/Late Intermediate Level
00296923 5 Solos..$8.99

WATERCOLOR MINIATURES
Early Intermediate Level
00296848 7 Solos..$7.99

JENNIFER LINN

AMERICAN IMPRESSIONS
Intermediate Level
00296471 6 Solos..$7.99

ANIMALS HAVE FEELINGS TOO
Early Elementary/Elementary Level
00147789 8 Solos..$7.99

CHRISTMAS IMPRESSIONS
Intermediate Level
00296706 8 Solos..$7.99

JUST PINK
Elementary Level
00296722 9 Solos..$7.99

LES PETITES IMAGES
Late Elementary Level
00296664 7 Solos..$7.99

LES PETITES IMPRESSIONS
Intermediate Level
00296355 6 Solos..$7.99

REFLECTIONS
Late Intermediate Level
00296843 5 Solos..$7.99

TALES OF MYSTERY
Intermediate Level
00296769 6 Solos..$8.99

MONA REJINO

CIRCUS SUITE
Late Elementary Level
00296665 5 Solos..$5.95

JUST FOR KIDS
Elementary Level
00296840 8 Solos..$7.99

MERRY CHRISTMAS MEDLEYS
Intermediate Level
00296799 5 Solos..$7.99

MINIATURES IN STYLE
Intermediate Level
00148088 6 Solos..$7.99

PORTRAITS IN STYLE
Early Intermediate Level
00296507 6 Solos..$7.99

For full descriptions and song lists, and to view a complete list of titles in this series, please visit **www.halleonard.com**

EUGÉNIE ROCHEROLLE

ENCANTOS ESPAÑOLES (SPANISH DELIGHTS)
Intermediate Level
00125451 6 Solos..$7.99

JAMBALAYA
FOR 2 PIANOS, 8 HANDS
Intermediate Level
00296654 Piano Ensemble............................$9.99

JAMBALAYA
FOR 2 PIANOS, 4 HANDS
Intermediate Level
00296725 Piano Duo (2 Pianos) $7.95

TOUR FOR TWO
Late Elementary Level
00296832 6 Duets.......................................$7.99

TREASURES
Late Elementary/Early Intermediate Level
00296924 7 Solos..$8.99

CHRISTOS TSITSAROS

DANCES FROM AROUND THE WORLD
Early Intermediate Level
00296688 7 Solos..$6.95

LYRIC BALLADS
Intermediate/Late Intermediate Level
00102404 6 Solos..$8.99

POETIC MOMENTS
Intermediate Level
00296403 8 Solos..$8.99

SONATINA HUMORESQUE
Late Intermediate Level
00296772 3 Movements $6.99

SONGS WITHOUT WORDS
Intermediate Level
00296506 9 Solos..$7.95

THREE PRELUDES
Early Advanced Level
00130747 ....$8.99

THROUGHOUT THE YEAR
Late Elementary Level
00296723 12 Duets......................................$6.95

ADDITIONAL COLLECTIONS

ALASKA SKETCHES
by Lynda Lybeck-Robinson
Early Intermediate Level
00119637 8 Solos..$7.99

AMERICAN PORTRAITS
by Wendy Stevens
Intermediate Level
00296817 6 Solos..$7.99

AN AWESOME ADVENTURE
by Lynda Lybeck-Robinson
Late Elementary Level
00137563..$7.99

AT THE LAKE
by Elvina Pearce
Elementary/Late Elementary Level
00131642 10 Solos and Duets......................$7.99

COUNTY RAGTIME FESTIVAL
by Fred Kern
Intermediate Level
00296882 7 Rags...$7.99

MYTHS AND MONSTERS
by Jeremy Siskind
Late Elementary/Early Intermediate Level
00148148 9 Solos..$7.99

PLAY THE BLUES!
by Luann Carman (Method Book)
Early Intermediate Level
00296357 10 Solos......................................$9.99

HAL•LEONARD®
CORPORATION
7777 W. BLUEMOUND RD. P.O. BOX 13819 MILWAUKEE, WI 53213